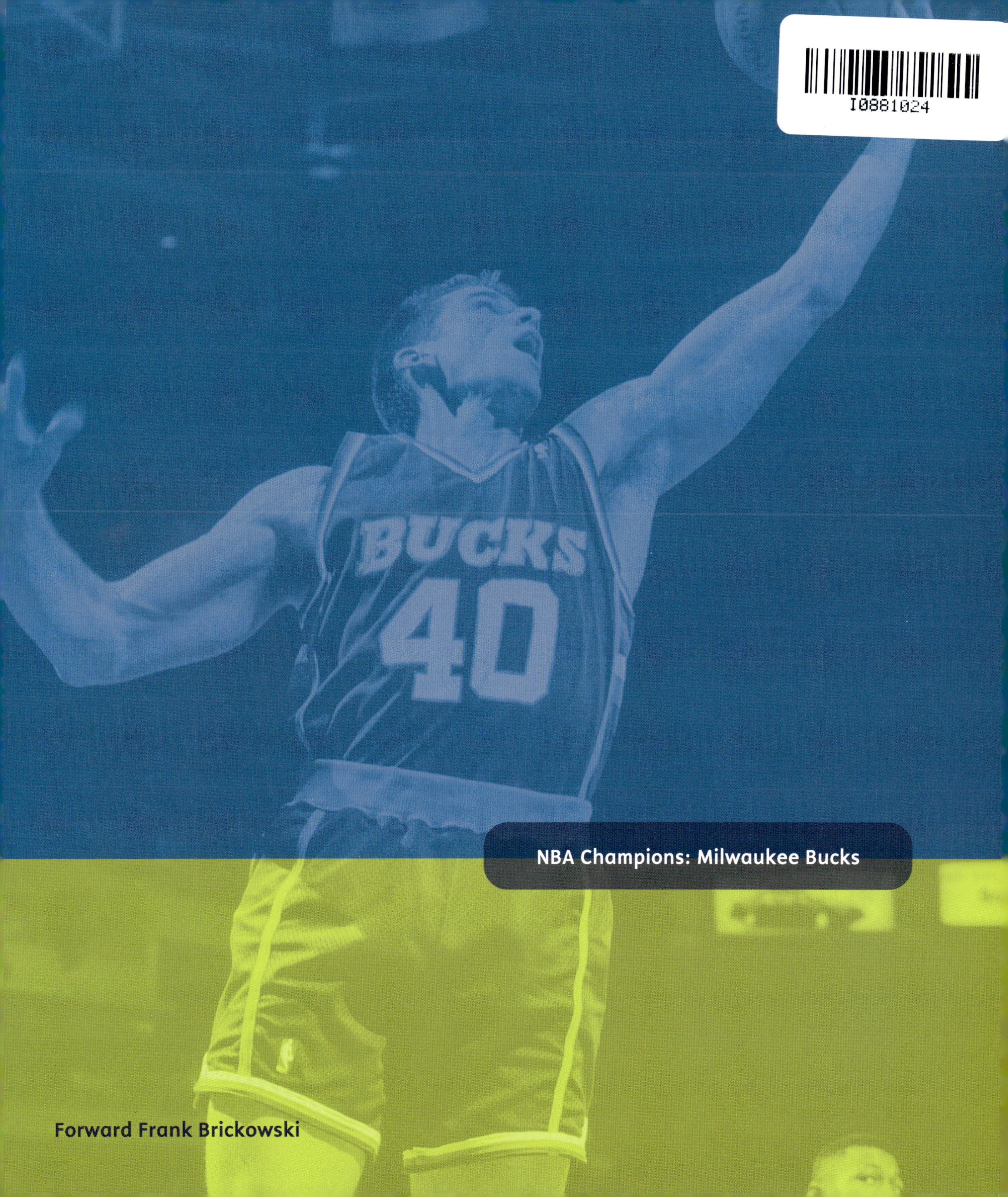

NBA Champions: Milwaukee Bucks

Forward Frank Brickowski

Shooting guard Sidney Moncrief

NBA CHAMPIONS

MILWAUKEE BUCKS

BY JAMES BARRY

CREATIVE SPORTS

CREATIVE EDUCATION / CREATIVE PAPERBACKS

Center Kareem Abdul-Jabbar

Published by Creative Education and Creative Paperbacks
P.O. Box 227, Mankato, Minnesota 56002
Creative Education and Creative Paperbacks are imprints of
The Creative Company
www.thecreativecompany.us

Art Direction by Tom Morgan
Book production by Graham Morgan
Edited by Grace Cain

Images by Getty Images/ Bettmann, 12, Brian Babineau, 6, Elsa, 16, Ezra Shaw, cover, Focus On Sport, cover, 7, 2, Jonathan Daniel, 19, 24, Mike McGinnis, 10, Paul Natkin, 15, Ronald C. Modra, 5, Stacy Revere, 20, Vernon Biever, 4; Newscom/ Harry E. Walker, 3; Steve Lipofsky, 1; Unsplash/ Wei Zeng, 9

Library of Congress Cataloging-in-Publication Data

Names: Barry, James (author of children's books), author.
Title: Milwaukee Bucks / by James Barry.
Description: Mankato, Minnesota : Creative Education and Creative Paperbacks, [2025] | Series: Creative sports. NBA champions | ATOS: 3.6. | Audience: Ages 7-10 years | Audience: Grades 2-3 | Summary: "Elementary-level text and dynamic sports photos highlight the NBA championship wins of the Milwaukee Bucks, plus sensational players associated with the professional basketball team such as Giannis Antetokounmpo"— Provided by publisher.
Identifiers: LCCN 2024014688 (print) | LCCN 2024014689 (ebook) | ISBN 9798889892601 (lib. bdg.) | ISBN 9781682776261 (paperback) | ISBN 9798889893714 (ebook)
Subjects: LCSH: Milwaukee Bucks (Basketball team)—Juvenile literature. | Basketball—Wisconsin—Milwaukee—History—Juvenile literature.
Classification: LCC GV885.52.M54 B37 2025 (print) | LCC GV885.52.M54 (ebook) | DDC 796.323/640977595—dc23/eng/20240423
LC record available at https://lccn.loc.gov/2024014688
LC ebook record available at https://lccn.loc.gov/2024014689

Printed in China

Center Bob Lanier

Point guard Brandon Jennings

CONTENTS

Home of the Bucks

Milwaukee, Wisconsin, is a snowy city during the Midwest's winter months. It is well known for its breweries and music festivals. The city is home to a new **arena** called the Fiserv Forum. Basketball fans go there on many cold nights. They cheer for a team called the Bucks.

Forward Giannis Antetokounmpo

MILWAUKEE BUCKS

The Milwaukee Bucks are part of the National Basketball Association (NBA). They play in the Central Division. That's part of the Eastern Conference. Two of the Bucks' biggest **rivals** are the Indiana Pacers and the Chicago Bulls. Teams in the NBA try to win the NBA Finals and become champions.

Point guard Flynn Robinson

Naming the Bucks

A contest was held to name the new team. Some top picks were Robins, Bucks, and even Skunks. Bucks was chosen. A buck is a male deer. There are many high-jumping, fast-moving deer in the Wisconsin woods. Team owners hoped their players would jump high and move fast too.

Bucks History

The Bucks started playing in 1968. They quickly became champions. They had two of the best players ever! In 1971, high-scoring center Kareem Abdul-Jabbar and **versatile** guard Oscar Robertson led the Bucks to a **title**. They reached the NBA Finals again in 1974. But they lost to the Boston Celtics.

Coach Don Nelson joined the Bucks later in the 1970s. He helped the team win 50 or more games for 7 years in a row. The Bucks made the **playoffs**

Center Kareem Abdul-Jabbar

Forward Giannis Antetokounmpo

each of those years. But they could not get back to the Finals.

In 2013, the Bucks made a great decision. They chose Giannis Antetokounmpo with the 15th pick in the NBA Draft. He is an excellent scorer, rebounder, and defender. Antetokounmpo won back-to-back **Most Valuable Player (MVP)** awards. In 2021, he led the Bucks to their second championship!

Other Bucks Stars

Milwaukee has had many great players. Scoring forward Marques Johnson was an **all-star** four times with the Bucks. Sidney Moncrief won back-to-back NBA Defensive Player of the Year awards.

Hot-shooting guard Ray Allen and high-scoring forward Glenn "Big Dog" Robinson led the team to the playoffs three years in a row. They almost

Shooting guard Ray Allen

Point guard Damian Lillard

made it back to the Finals in 2001. Lefty shooting guard Michael Redd was a top scorer in the 2000s. He was an all-star with the Bucks.

In 2023, exciting guard Damian Lillard teamed up with Antetokounmpo and joined the Bucks. Fans hope the team's new superstar duo will lead them to a third championship!

About the Bucks

First season: 1968–69

Conference/division: Eastern Conference, Central Division

Team colors: Good Land green, Cream City cream, Great Lakes blue, black, and white

Home arena: Fiserv Forum

NBA CHAMPIONSHIPS:

1971, 4 games to 0 over Baltimore Bullets

2021, 4 games to 2 over Phoenix Suns

TEAM WEBSITE:

https://www.nba.com/bucks/

Glossary

all-star—a player picked to play in the All-Star Game, featuring the season's top stars

arena—a large building with seats for spectators, where sports games and entertainment events are held

Most Valuable Player (MVP)—an honor given to the season's best player

playoffs—games that the best teams play after a regular season to see who the champion will be

rival—a team that plays extra hard against another team

title—another word for championship

versatile—able to do many different things well

Forward Khris Middleton

Index